SHAKER COOKING

Introduced by Bobbie Crosby
Designed by Alison Jewell
Photographed by Peter Barry
Recipes styled by Helen Burdett
Edited by Jillian Stewart

All recipes are reprinted by kind permission of Macmillan
Publishing Co., Inc., 866 Third Avenue, New York, N.Y. 10022 from
The Best of Shaker Cooking by Amy Bess Miller and Persis Fuller,
copyright 1970 by Shaker Community, Inc.

CLB 2379
This 1991 edition published by Crescent Books,
distributed by Outlet Book Company Inc., a Random House Company,
225 Park Avenue South, New York, New York 10003.
Color separations by Scantrans Pte Ltd, Singapore.
Printed and bound in Singapore.
ISBN 0 517 05150 8
8 7 6 5 4 3 2 1

SHAKER COOKING

CRESCENT BOOKS
NEW YORK

INTRODUCTION

I live in a Shaker house. Or, rather, my house was originally built by Shakers in the North Family settlement in Tyringham Valley in western Massachusetts. I make the distinction because the house is not what it once was. Since its construction 200 years ago, various owners including myself, have altered the original simple wooden home built on a stone foundation. In the late nineteenth century somebody added porches. Later, a large addition was built on the south end. My husband and I this winter added yet another addition on the north side.

Sometimes I wish I could view the original house; the way it looked when the finishing touches were first completed. I've looked for original pictures or drawings of the house but to no avail. I can only imagine. I picture a simple, yet elegant house. There is a mammoth stone chimney built carefully with the finest stones. It was made to last and it has. The wooden floor is made out of two-foot-wide planks of pine. You can't buy that kind of wood now (or at least I can't). Simplicity. Quality. Austerity. And quality. That's what I see at the core of my house. Did I mention quality?

I don't think we diminished it with our post-Shaker additions, but we did change it. Shaker furniture was beautiful but sparse. Their clothing was uniform. Their lives were separate and celibate. All that has changed with the advent of modern times. Simplicity and purity have been made more complicated.

When I look at the Shaker recipes featured in this book I see that simplicity and purity all over again. It is as if I get to see my original home. There is one catch though. Unlike the architecture. Unlike the furniture. And unlike their social lives, austerity played a limited role for the Shakers when it came to eating. Food was the one exception. They allowed themselves one bit of self-indulgence – what they ate and how they prepared it. A typical meal was described as "bread and butter, pye, strawberry sauce, fried potatoes, fresh meat, stewed beans and green tea sweetened with leaf sugar." Not bad for a self-denying society. They ate doughnuts, beefsteak, and lobster. They enjoyed seasoned foods and looked forward every spring to the gathering of strawberries and fresh vegetables. They grew herbs and used them in every conceivable way. They loved their cream and used it in many of their sauces.

Unfortunately, the eating habits in the Shaker ministries were very self-indulgent and during the mid 1830s there was a movement to eliminate all meat, liquor (which they did drink), tea and coffee from their diet. For 15 years pork was prohibited by "devine instruction" and many ministries only allowed vegetarian meals to be served. The reasoning was not only moralistic, but practical as well. By eliminating meat, tea and coffee, meals would be less expensive. The theory was that it would also eliminate the sexual tension among the young. Whatever the rationale, it was too much to give up and by 1855, the dietary restrictions were done away with and the United Society could once again enjoy caffeine and meat, including pork.

Today, Shaker food as we know it is a collection of carefully researched recipes recorded and passed from generation to generation. We find what once worked in the communal kitchen of the ministries works just as well in the world of mixers and microwaves. The wonderful simplicity and ease of preparation, and adaptability of Shaker cooking is what makes it so special. I came to realize how special when I was hired by Hancock Shaker Village to prepare all the meals served at "An Evening at Hancock Shaker Village's Candlelight Dinner and Tour." This is a series of events held throughout the year. And as the Shaker women did, I and my staff prepared food for the many guests who gathered at the long tables to eat dinner family-style as the Shakers did so many years ago.

Today, Shaker food is comfort food and more. The subtle use of herbs and fruits combined with meats and vegetables makes it both fresh tasting and refreshing. The traditional choice of ingredients makes it timeless and unintimidating. It is a very special legacy, a legacy that allows us to share one of the few luxuries the Shakers allowed themselves – the gift of wonderful food.

Bobbie Crosby
Tyringham, Massachusetts

Corn Chowder

HANCOCK SHAKER VILLAGE

Serves 6

Ingredients

4 tablespoons diced salt pork
1 tablespoon butter
1 medium onion, sliced
3 potatoes, peeled and finely diced
2 cups chicken stock
2 cups corn scraped from the cob *or*

2 cups home canned corn
(called home style)
4 cups whole milk
Salt and pepper
1 cup heavy cream
3 tablespoons butter

Fry salt pork in butter, remove pieces when crispy and reserve. Add onion to fat and sauté until golden. Add potatoes and stock and cook slowly until soft. Add corn and milk, lower heat, and simmer until corn is tender. Young corn takes 5 minutes. (Dried corn which has been freshened will take longer.) Add salt and pepper. Bring to boil and remove from heat. Add cream and butter. Stir up well and pour into soup plates or tureen. Float pork on top.

Previous page: Mt. Lebanon Shaker village, New York. Above: the Shakers sold their high quality produce to the outside world with much success.

Tomato Soup

SISTER OLIVE, HANCOCK SHAKER VILLAGE

Serves 10

Ingredients

½ teaspoon baking soda
1 quart very ripe tomatoes, peeled
2 quarts whole milk
1 teaspoon salt
1 teaspoon pepper

1 teaspoon mace
1 teaspoon sugar
2 tablespoons butter
8 saltines, finely crushed

Add soda to tomatoes, mash and stew until they are completely cooked. Boil milk. Add tomatoes and stir well. Boil together, with seasonings, for 5 minutes. Add butter and just before serving thicken with finely crushed crackers.

Above: Shaker clothing and utensils reflect the practical nature of the Shaker lifestyle.

Cream of Asparagus Soup

HANCOCK SHAKER VILLAGE

Serves 4

Ingredients

1 pound fresh asparagus
2 cups water
1 small onion, thinly sliced
1½ cups chicken stock
2 tablespoons butter

2 tablespoons flour
2 cups scalded milk
½ cup cream
Salt and pepper

Cut asparagus free of tough ends. Cut 2-inch tips off and reserve. Cut remainder of stalks into small pieces, cover with water, bring to boil and cook 10 minutes uncovered. Add onion and chicken stock and cook to reduce still further. Remove from fire and force through sieve. Make thickening by melting butter, adding flour and hot milk. Cook for 5 minutes, stirring to keep smooth. Add to sieved pulp. Heat and remove from stove. Add cream and seasonings and tips.

Above: the Shakers were ingenious craftsmen who made all their own implements.

Shaker Baked Fish with Herb Dressing

MARY WHITCHER'S SHAKER HOUSEKEEPER

Serves 4

Ingredients

1 whole fish (2 pounds), cleaned
6 soda crackers, crushed
1 teaspoon salt
1 teaspoon pepper
1 teaspoon sugar
1 tablespoon minced parsley
1 tablespoon minced thyme

1 tablespoon powdered cloves
1 tablespoon butter
Fish broth to moisten
4 strips salt pork
Salt and pepper
Corn meal for dredging

Scrap fish well and wash; remove head and tail in water, cover fish in water which will be used as fish broth. Make a dressing of crushed crackers, salt, pepper, sugar, minced herbs and butter. Moisten with fish broth. Stuff fish and fasten with wooden skewers. Place in buttered baking dish and cut a few shallow slashes across fish. Lay on thin strips of salt pork and dredge with salt, pepper, and corn meal. Bake in slow oven (325°F) for 1½ hours. Serve on hot platter surrounded with tomato sauce and wedges of lemon or horse-radish sauce.

Above: Hancock Shaker Village in Massachusetts with its impressive round barn in the foreground. Built in 1826, it is a marvel of efficient Shaker design.

Scalloped Oysters

MANUSCRIPT FROM MT. LEBANON SHAKER VILLAGE

Serves 8

Ingredients

4 cups grated bread	Pepper
1 quart shelled oysters	2 cups butter
Mace	3 tablespoons sherry

Grate the bread, wash and scald the oysters, drain quite dry, reserving liquid. Put a thin layer of bread upon the bottom and sides of a 2 quart baking dish, then alternate a layer of oysters and bread and season well with mace and pepper. The butter is added in small pieces with each layer of oysters and upon the top. Two layers of oysters is enough in order to cook all well. Add the liquor hot and sherry, then a top layer of crumbs. Bake in a preheated oven 425°F for 20-25 minutes until golden brown on top.

We use the English sherry, but this is left to individual preference.

Above: the Shakers at Pleasant Hill, Kentucky raised sheep and produced excellent cloth after a long process involving carding, spinning and weaving.

Oysters and Sausage

SHIRLEY SHAKER VILLAGE

Serves 4

Ingredients

1½ cups white flour

3 teaspoons baking powder

½ teaspoon salt

1 tablespoon butter

1 cup drained chopped oysters

6 tablespoons oyster liquor

8 pork sausages

Sift flour, baking powder, and salt together. Cut in butter as for pastry. To this mixture add oysters and their liquor, blend together, and spread in a buttered, shallow baking pan. On top arrange sausages, which have been cooked for 10 minutes in boiling water. Bake for 30 minutes in a 350°F oven. Turn sausages once to brown.

Above: an interpretive craftsman demonstrates how the Shakers made metal hoops for water dippers at Pleasant Hill, Kentucky.

Curried Swordfish Hancock Style

HANCOCK SHAKER VILLAGE

Should serve 5-6

Ingredients

2 slices swordfish (4 x 8 inches in size and 1½-inches thick weighing 3 pounds in all or more)
3 cups boiling water
1 teaspoon salt
½ teaspoon black pepper
1 bay leaf

1 tablespoon lemon juice
3 tablespoons butter
1 tablespoon chopped onion
2 tablespoons flour
1 teaspoon curry powder
¼ cup light cream
Paprika

Place swordfish slices in large frying pan and cover with boiling water. Add salt, pepper, bay leaf, and lemon juice. Simmer uncovered over low heat for 15 minutes, until just tender. With a wide spatula lift fish out of stock and place on ovenproof platter or in a shallow casserole, and keep warm.

Strain stock. Measure out 1½ cups. Melt butter in saucepan and sauté onion in it until limp. Blend in flour. Gradually pour in the strained stock and cook until thickened. Blend in curry powder and cream. Pour sauce over fish slices, sprinkle with paprika, slip under preheated broiler for 5 minutes to brown lightly. Cut into serving portions.

Above: the Cooper's building at Shakertown, Pleasant Hill, illustrates the neatness, simplicity and elegant proportions so representative of Shaker architecture.

Chicken Cutlets with Chopped Mushroom Sauce

HANCOCK SHAKER VILLAGE

Makes 10 little cutlets and 4 cups of sauce

Ingredients

½ cup butter	Salt, pepper, nutmeg to taste
½ cup flour	4 cups finely minced cooked chicken
½ cup milk	Very fine breadcrumbs
1 teaspoon chopped onion	1 egg, beaten
2 teaspoons chopped parsley	Lard and butter, half and half

Combine ½ cup butter and ½ cup flour, cook slowly for 5 minutes. Add milk, onion, parsley, and seasonings; cook until quite thick. Add chicken. Mix well and put on a platter to cool. Handle quickly. Shape into small cutlets. Roll in breadcrumbs, then in beaten egg, then again in breadcrumbs. Fry to a golden brown in hot fat, half lard and half butter. Serve with Mushroom Sauce.

Mushroom Sauce

4 cups chopped mushrooms	2 tablespoons thick, homemade catsup
2 tablespoons chopped onions	1 teaspoon Herb Vinegar
4 tablespoons butter	2 tablespoons heavy cream

Combine mushrooms, onions, and butter and sauté well until mushrooms and onions are both very tender and dark. Add catsup and Herb Vinegar and continue cooking another 10 minutes, slowly. It should bubble. Remove from heat and add cream. Stir briskly. Do not reheat. Pour around the cutlets or serve in sauceboat.

Above: part of the Shaker village at Mt. Lebanon. Founded in 1787 it was the first gathering of Shakers into a separate community.

Chicken In Heavy Cream

HANCOCK SHAKER VILLAGE

Serves 4

Ingredients

1 small chicken, young and tender
2 tablespoons sweet butter
1 tablespoon flour
1 medium-size onion
4 whole cloves
1 teaspoon salt
1/2 teaspoon white pepper

2 tablespoons tarragon sprigs
(do not chop since sprigs must
eventually be removed)
2 tablespoons butter
2 tablespoons flour
1 cup heavy cream

Sauté chicken in melted butter but do not brown. Add onion with cloves stuck in it, salt, pepper, and sprigs of tarragon. Pour over hot water, barely to cover, and cook, covered, for 20 to 30 minutes until chicken is tender. Remove chicken to a hot platter in oven. Remove tarragon from stock in skillet. Melt the remaining butter in a separate pan, add flour and cook gently for 1 minute. Gradually stir in 1 cup of the chicken stock and cook until thickened, then stir in the heavy cream and mix thoroughly. Pour hot sauce over chicken.

Above: Pleasant Hill Shaker village in Kentucky has been carefully restored and can now be seen at its former glory, complete with costumed interpreters and craftsmen.

Corned Beef and Cabbage

HANCOCK SHAKER VILLAGE

Serves 4-6

Ingredients

4 pounds corned beef	6 carrots
1 tablespoon brown sugar	6 onions studded with cloves
6 potatoes, peeled	Salt
6 turnips	1 medium cabbage, quartered

Soak choice brisket of corned beef in cold water for an hour. Drain and cover with fresh cold water and bring to a boil. Skim well. Put pot on low heat, add tablespoon of brown sugar and let meat simmer partially covered very gently for 4 hours; 30 minutes before meat is done, boil in a separate pot, the peeled potatoes, turnips, carrots, and onions, salted lightly. In still another pot cook the cut cabbage for 15 minutes. Lift the brisket onto a large, well-heated platter and surround with the cooked vegetables. Serve with fresh horse-radish or mustard. Any sauce served with this dish should be tart because the vegetables are sweet.

Above: the sheer size of some of the Shaker houses testifies to the woodworking talents of the Brothers within the Shaker communities.

Minted Lamb Shanks

HANCOCK SHAKER VILLAGE

Serves 4

Ingredients

4 lamb shanks
Salt and pepper
Flour
1 cup water
¹/₂ cup pitted prunes,
    soaked and cooked
¹/₂ cup dried apricots,
    soaked and cooked

1 tablespoon chopped parsley
1 tablespoon brown sugar
¹/₂ teaspoon cinnamon
¹/₂ teaspoon allspice
¹/₄ teaspoon cloves
3 tablespoons vinegar
¹/₄ teaspoon salt
1 tablespoon chopped mint

Season meat with salt and pepper, dredge with flour, and place in large
(4 quart) greased baking dish. Cover and bake in moderate 375°F oven until
meat is tender, 1³/₄ to 2 hours. Combine remaining ingredients, heat to boiling,
and simmer for about 5 minutes. Draw most of fat from cooked shanks, add
fruit mixture to meat, cover and bake at 400°F for 30 minutes.

Above: the Shakers made their own boxes in a wide range of sizes and seed boxes in
particular were important for their commercial seed industry.

Liver Baked with Onions and Herbs

THE MANIFESTO

Serves 6

Ingredients

1 large onion, sliced
2 tablespoons melted butter
¼ cup hot water
6 slices liver (calf, veal, or beef),
   cut ½-inch thick
2 tablespoons flour, seasoned
   with salt and pepper

1 tablespoon chopped parsley
2 teaspoons thyme
2 tablespoons thick chili sauce
1 tablespoon brown sugar
2 tablespoons butter

Place onion in oven pan, pour over it butter and water. Cover and bake in moderate 350°F oven for 30 minutes. Dredge liver in flour; arrange over onions, sprinkle with parsley and thyme and dot with chili sauce, sugar, and butter. Bake covered for 30 minutes at 350°F and then uncovered until liver is browned.

Above: the furniture gallery at the Shaker Museum, Old Chatham, New York, has a wealth of beautiful, functional furniture all hand-made by the Shakers.

Roast Pork

HANCOCK SHAKER VILLAGE

Serves 4

Ingredients

4 pound loin of pork
1 clove garlic, sliced
Salt and pepper
4 tablespoons melted butter
1 cup sweet cider

1 cup applesauce
2 apples, cored, pared and sliced thin
$1/2$-$3/4$ cup brown sugar
$1/2$ cup heavy cream

Tie roast is needed to hold shape. Pierce here and there and insert bits of garlic in the holes. Rub with salt and pepper. Place fat side up in an open roasting pan. Sear in a very hot oven at 450°F for 30 minutes, basting now and then with a mixture of fat in the pan, butter, and cider. After 30 minutes reduce the heat to 350°F and roast meat for another hour, basting often with drippings. Remove from oven and pour off about three-quarters of the fat in the pan. Spread roast with apple-sauce and arrange apple slices sprinkled with brown sugar around the roast in the pan. Return to the oven and roast about 1 hour longer, basting frequently. Add cream to pan gravy before serving. Serve gravy separately.

If cider is not available, apple juice or dry white wine can be substituted.

Above: this view of Pleasant Hill, Kentucky illustrates the neatness and simplicity
central to the Shaker lifestyle.

Pork Chops with Mustard

MT. LEBANON SHAKER VILLAGE

Serves 4

Ingredients
4 thick pork chops (rib or loin)
2 tablespoons butter
$\frac{1}{2}$ cup cider
1 teaspoon mustard

Salt and pepper
$\frac{1}{2}$ cup heavy cream
2 tablespoons parsley, finely chopped

In a large skillet fry the chops very slowly in the butter until brown on both sides. This should take 30 to 40 minutes, keeping the pan covered. Add cider and cook for 10 minutes longer if necessary. This depends on the thickness of the chops. Chops should be tender. Pork needs slow, long cooking.

Remove chops to heated platter and keep warm. Add the mustard, seasonings and cream to liquid in fry pan; heat up. Pour over chops, garnish with parsley, and serve at once.

Above: a portrait of Canterbury Sister Emma Neal. (*Photograph courtesy of the Shaker Museum, Old Chatham, New York.*)

Shaker Flank Steak

HANCOCK SHAKER VILLAGE

Serves 6

Ingredients

3 pounds round beef,
   cut 1½-inches thick
2 tablespoons flour
2 tablespoons butter
1 teaspoon salt
¼ teaspoon pepper

1 stalk celery, chopped
1 carrot, chopped fine
½ green pepper, chopped fine
2 medium onions, chopped fine
Juice ½ lemon
½ cup catsup

Cut or score both sides of the meat diagonally and dust with flour. Sauté in heated butter until well browned on both sides. Season with salt and pepper, then add all the chopped vegetables. Last of all, add lemon juice and catsup. Cover tightly and simmer very gently for 1 to 1½ hours, or until the steak is tender when tested with a fork. The vegetables cook down to a rich sauce to be served with the meat.

Above: many Shaker communities successfully traded dried herbs, utilizing the broad green spaces around their villages to plant herb gardens.

Ham Baked in Cider

MARY WHITCHER'S SHAKER HOUSEKEEPER

Serves 12

Ingredients

11 pound ham	2 tablespoons brown sugar
24 whole cloves	2 small onions
1 cup boiling water	1 tablespoon lemon juice
4 cups apple cider	1 tablespoon flour, browned

Scrub ham thoroughly and soak overnight in cold water. If the ham has been precooked, it will be ready for baking. If not, put in cold water and bring to a rapid boil; reduce heat, cover and simmer for 3 hours. Let cool in liquid. Remove rind and trim fat; score and stud with cloves. Combine boiling water, cider, brown sugar, and onions and boil for 10 minutes. Strain and pour over ham in roaster and bake for 1 hour in moderate 350°F oven, basting every 15 minutes. Remove ham from roaster and strain liquid; add lemon juice and thicken with browned flour. Serve this as a sauce with the ham.

Above: Shaker furniture has become much sought after, its clean lines and functional nature endearing it to a growing number of people world wide.

Veal Chops

MANUSCRIPT FROM SHAKER MUSEUM, OLD CHATHAM, NEW YORK

Serves 4

Ingredients

4 tablespoons butter

2 tablespoons chicken fat

4 veal chops about 1-inch thick

4 tablespoons chopped onion

4 tablespoons flour

1 cup cider

1 cup cream

Salt and pepper

1 tablespoon chopped parsley

In 2 tablespoons of the butter and 2 tablespoon of chicken fat, fry chops until they are golden on both sides. Remove to ovenproof baking dish and keep warm. Add remaining butter to fat in skillet and cook chopped onions. When soft, add flour. Cook for 1 minute, stirring. Add cider and cook until sauce is thick and smooth. Add cream and seasonings. Pour sauce over chops in oven and cook until tender. This may take 25 minutes at 350°F, or more, depending on tenderness of meat. Garnish with parsley.

Above: amongst many other duties, the women were responsible for making all the cloth for the members of their community.

Pleasant Hill Baked Eggplant

SHAKERTOWN, PLEASANT HILL

Serves 4

Ingredients

1 large eggplant
Salt
½ medium onion
2 tablespoons butter
3 tablespoons chopped parsley

2 cups stewed mushrooms
Worcestershire sauce (to season)
Pepper
1½ cups cracker crumbs
2 tablespoons butter

Cut eggplant in half lengthwise, scrape out inside, leaving ¼ inch around sides and bottom of shell. Take eggplant meat and parboil in salt water until it is tender. Drain thoroughly and chop roughly. Sauté the onion in the butter and add chopped parsley. Mix eggplant and onion-parsley mixture with stewed mushrooms. Season with Worcestershire sauce, salt, and pepper. Add 1 cup cracker crumbs. Place in eggplant shell. Sprinkle top with remaining crumbs and dot with butter. Bake at 375°F for 30 to 35 minutes.

Above: the Shaker village at Mt. Lebanon, New York, is open to visitors, although part of it now houses a preparatory school.

Rice Croquettes, White, Brown, or Wild

WATERVLIET SHAKER VILLAGE, NEW YORK

Serves 6

Ingredients

1 cup rice, white, brown, or wild
3 cups rich chicken broth
4 egg yolks, beaten
2 teaspoons onion juice or
  scraped onion pulp
1 teaspoon each finely chopped
  parsley and chives

2 tablespoons chopped nuts (optional)
Salt and pepper
2 eggs, beaten
1 tablespoon milk
1 cup sieved dry breadcrumbs
Hot fat

Wash rice. Cook in chicken broth, uncovered, for about 30 minutes, or until rice is tender and all liquid has been absorbed. Stir in beaten egg yolks, onion juice, parsley, chives, nuts, and seasonings. Mix well. Cool and chill.

Form rice mixture into croquettes, dip in mixture of beaten egg and milk, then roll in very fine, sieved, dry breadcrumbs. Chill the croquettes until ready to serve. Fry 3 croquettes at a time in hot fat in a deep skillet for about 2 minutes or until golden. Drain on absorbent paper. Serve with or without a sauce.

Above: Sabbathday Lake, Maine, was founded in 1794 and is one of the smallest and most isolated of the Shaker settlements.

Green Bean Casserole

SHAKER FESTIVAL, AUBURN, KENTUCKY

Serves 8

Ingredients
3 tablespoons butter, melted
2 tablespoons flour
1 teaspoon salt
¼ teaspoon pepper
1 teaspoon sugar

½ medium-sized onion, grated
1 cup sour cream
1½ pounds fresh green beans
½ pound grated Cheddar cheese
½ cup breadcrumbs

Combine 2 tablespoons butter and flour and cook gently; remove from heat; stir in seasonings, onions, and cream, fold in beans. Place in shallow 2 quart casserole. Cover with cheese; then with crumbs, mixed with 1 tablespoon butter. Bake in moderate 350°F oven for 30 minutes, then brown under a preheated broiler until golden and crispy.

Above: the Pleasant Hill Shakers were excellent basket makers, producing a variety of shapes and sizes for their own use.

Green and Red Cabbage

HANCOCK SHAKER VILLAGE

Serves 4-6

Ingredients

½ head red cabbage	1 teaspoon salt
½ head green cabbage	¼ cup boiling water
2 tablespoons finely chopped onion	4 tablespoons brown sugar
3 tablespoons butter	4 tablespoons vinegar
2 tart apples	1 teaspoon chopped chives or basil

Remove outer leaves from cabbage. Shred, rinse in cold water, drain but do not dry. Sauté onion for 3 minutes in butter. Combine cabbage and onion. Cook, covered, for 10 minutes. Peel and core apples, cut into fine pieces. Add to cabbage and onion mixture. Add salt and boiling water. Mix well. Simmer, covered for 30 minutes or until cabbage is tender. Add brown sugar and vinegar. Simmer for 10 minutes longer. Add chopped chives or basil.

Above: much of the Shaker women's time was taken up with spinning wool which they dyed using natural vegetable dyes.

Carrots Cooked in Honey

ENFIELD SHAKER VILLAGE, CONNECTICUT

Serves 4

Ingredients

3 cups round carrots, 1/4-inch thick	1/2 cup honey
3 tablespoons butter	1/2 teaspoon salt
1/2 cup chicken broth	1/4 teaspoon pepper

Cook carrots in butter and chicken broth for 5 minutes with cover on saucepan. Remove lid, add honey and seasonings and cook until carrots are tender, about 15 minutes.

Above: a woman prepares medicines at Canterbury Shaker Village, New Hampshire.(*Photograph courtesy of The Shaker Museum, Old Chatham, New York.*)

Onion Pie

SHIRLEY SHAKER VILLAGE

Serves 6

Ingredients

4 cups thinly sliced onions
3 tablespoons butter
Pepper and salt
Nutmeg

6-8 ounces pastry
2 eggs
½ cup sour cream mixed with
    2 tablespoons sweet cream

Sauté onions slowly in butter until soft but not brown. Season highly with pepper, salt, and nutmeg. Line a deep pie pan with pastry. Beat the eggs lightly, fold into the onions. Add onions to pastry-lined tin. Top with sour cream mixture. Bake in 350°F oven for 30 minutes or until top is golden brown.

Above: Shakertown at Pleasant Hill, Kentucky, is a living museum where visitors can watch craftsmen recreate the scenes which once took place in Shaker workshops.

Shaker Squash

MT. LEBANON SHAKER VILLAGE

Serves 6

Ingredients
4 pounds Hubbard squash, cut up
4 cups hot water
$^1/_2$ teaspoon salt

$^1/_2$ teaspoon pepper
3 tablespoons butter
$^1/_2$ cup maple syrup

Steam the squash in the hot water. Remove from shell when tender. Drain if necessary and discard seeds. Pass through sieve and season with salt, pepper, butter, and maple syrup. Beat well and heat before serving.

Variation: Put a whole Hubbard squash in a slow 300°F oven and bake for 2$^1/_2$ hours. Remove. It will now cut easily. Remove seeds and fiber. Divide into serving portions, place in pan and dust well with salt, pepper, and brown sugar and dot heavily with butter. Set under broiler to brown. Any remaining squash can be used for pies or puddings in place of pumpkin.

Above: the Shaker settlement on the shores of Mascoma Lake, New Hampshire has a fascinating range of hand-made implements on display.

Ginger Beets

HANCOCK SHAKER VILLAGE

Serves 8-10

Ingredients

2 cups sugar
6 tablespoons cornstarch
3 teaspoons ginger
6 cups small cooked beets
1 cup cider or ½ cup vinegar
    and ½ cup cider

1 tablespoon butter
½ teaspoon salt
1 cup seedless raisins

Combine sugar, cornstarch, and ginger; if there is some liquid from the cooked beets, perhaps a cup, add this with the vinegar and cider. If there is no liquid because the beets have been steamed, use an additional cup of cider. Bring to a boil, cook stirring constantly until thick and clear. Add butter, salt, and raisins, and lastly, beets. Heat thoroughly and serve.

Above: the interior of the schoolroom at Canterbury.(*Photograph courtesy of the Shaker Museum, Old Chatham, New York.*)

Herb Bread

HANCOCK SHAKER VILLAGE

Yields 2 loaves

Ingredients

2 cups milk
1/4 cup sugar
1/4 teaspoon salt
2 envelopes active dry yeast
2 eggs, well beaten
1 teaspoon powdered
   nutmeg or cloves

2 teaspoons crumbled,
   dried sage leaves
4 teaspoons caraway seeds
1 teaspoon dried rosemary
1 teaspoon dried dill
7 1/2-8 cups presifted flour
1/4 cup melted butter

Scald milk. Stir in sugar and salt, cool to lukewarm. Add yeast. Stir well until completely dissolved. Add eggs, nutmeg, herbs, caraway seeds and 4 cups of the flour. Beat until smooth. Add butter and enough of the remaining flour to make a soft dough that is easy to handle. Turn onto lightly floured board. Knead until smooth and elastic. Place dough in greased bowl, cover, and let rise for about 2 hours or until doubled in bulk. Grease 2 loaf pans. Punch dough down. Divide in half. Fill each pan, cover, let rise again, 1 hour or until doubled. Preheat oven to 425°F. Bake for 15 minutes. Reduce heat to 375°F. Bake for 35 minutes. A nice addition is 2 teaspoons of celery seeds.

Above: between 1787 and 1947 Mt. Lebanon Shaker Village was the center of the Shaker Ministry, which directed policy for Shakers nationwide.

Believers' Bread

HANCOCK SHAKER VILLAGE

Makes 4 one pound loaves

Ingredients

2 cups milk
1/4 cup granulated sugar
4 teaspoons salt
4 tablespoons butter
2 cups lukewarm water

2 cakes yeast or 2 envelopes
    active dry yeast
1/4 cup warm water
10 to 12 cups sifted all purpose flour
Melted butter

Scald milk, add sugar, salt, butter, and half the lukewarm water. Stir until sugar is dissolved and butter melted. Cool to lukewarm.

Soften yeast in remaining 1 1/4 cups water and add to milk mixture.

Add flour a cupful at a time, mixing thoroughly each time with a knife until the dough comes away from the bowl and can be turned out on a floured board and kneaded. Knead for 8 to 10 minutes. Shape dough into round ball, put in greased bowl and brush top with melted butter. Cover and let rise in warm place (80°-85°) away from drafts until it doubles in bulk. This will take from 2 to 2 1/2 hours. Knead down again, cover, and let rise again, until double in bulk, about 1 hour.

Turn dough out onto a floured board and knead well again. Cut into 4 equal portions. Round up each piece. Cover with a clean towel and let rise 10 to 15 minutes on board. Shape each ball into loaf form and place smooth side up in 4 greased pans. Brush lightly with melted butter. Cover with clean cloth and place in warm place (80°-85°). Let rise until double in bulk about 1 1/2 hours. Preheat oven to 400°F. Bake at 400°F for first 10 minutes and then at 350°F for 35 minutes. Brush with melted butter. Remove from pans and let cool on rack.

Takes about 7 hours – maybe less, to make.

This recipe can also be used to make rolls. To make rolls, shape as desired. Place in lightly greased 8 inch round layer cake pan or on lightly greased cooky sheet. Cover and let rise in warm place until doubled in size – about 35 minutes. Bake in 400°F oven for 15 to 20 minutes.

Variation: For whole wheat bread use 1/2 whole wheat flour and 1/2 white flour. For graham bread use 1/2 graham flour and 1/2 white flour.

Buttermilk Rolls

HANCOCK SHAKER VILLAGE

Makes about 2 dozen

Ingredients

1 envelope active dry yeast
1/4 cup warm water
1 1/2 cups lukewarm buttermilk
3 tablespoons sugar

1/2 cup melted shortening
4 1/2 cups sifted flour
1/2 teaspoon baking soda
1 teaspoon salt

In mixing bowl soften yeast in water. Add buttermilk, sugar, and shortening. In another bowl sift together dry ingredients. Stir into butter-milk mixture. Beat until smooth. Let stand for 10 minutes. Roll out dough. Shape into rolls; arrange on greased cooky sheet, cover, let rise for about 30 minutes. In preheated 400°F oven bake for 15 to 20 minutes.

Above: the Kentucky Shakers, like their counterparts in other states, used their idea of simplicity to build dwellings of honesty and beauty.

Apple Pancakes

HANCOCK SHAKER VILLAGE

Yields 10-12 cakes

Ingredients

2 cups sifted flour
1 teaspoon baking powder
½ teaspoon salt
1 teaspoon sugar

2 eggs, lightly beaten
1½ cups rich milk
2 tablespoons melted butter
½-1 cup peeled, finely chopped apple

Sift flour with other dry ingredients in mixing bowl. Add eggs and milk and beat to make smooth. Add butter and apples. Stir well. Grease a hot griddle for the first batch. Generally greasing is not necessary after that if recipe contains 2 tablespoons or more of fat. Griddle is at proper heat if when tested with drops of water, they do a lively dance.

After pancakes have browned sprinkle with cinnamon and sugar or pass cream flavored with cinnamon, or flavored with rose water.

Variation: For blueberry pancakes add ⅔ to 1 cup of berries. Serve with melted butter or maple syrup.

Above: A costumed interpreter prepares a meal at Pleasant Hill, Kentucky. Cooking for Shaker mealtimes was a large-scale task with many mouths to feed.

Honey Cake
With Almonds

NORTH UNION SHAKER VILLAGE, OHIO

Makes 1 cake

Ingredients

2³/₄ cups flour
¹/₂ teaspoon powdered cloves
1 teaspoon cinnamon
³/₄ teaspoon each grated nutmeg,
   cream tartar, baking soda
¹/₄ teaspoon salt
²/₃ cup butter, melted

1¹/₂ tablespoons lard, melted
3 tablespoons dark brown sugar
1 tablespoon white sugar
3 eggs, beaten
1¹/₂ cups honey
³/₄ cup sour cream
Blanched halved almonds

Sift together first five dry ingredients. Melt shortenings and add to them both sugars. Beat eggs until fluffy, add honey and sour cream and add the butter-sugar mixture to them, stirring vigorously. Gradually stir in dry ingredients. Turn batter into a buttered and floured 9-inch cake tin 2-inches deep and cover top at regular intervals with blanched, halved almonds. Bake cake in moderate 375°F oven for about 45 minutes, or until golden brown. Test center with straw or cake tester. If it comes out clean, the cake is done. Remove from pan to cake rack to cool. Put in tightly closed container to ripen for at least 2 days. It will keep for weeks.

Above: the Shakers were masters of many crafts and devised ingenious methods for making a whole range of necessities.

Sister Susan's Cream Layer Cake

HANCOCK SHAKER VILLAGE

Makes 1 cake

Ingredients
Note: *All ingredients must be at room temperature.*

$^3/_4$ cup butter

$^1/_2$ cup sugar

3 eggs

$^2/_3$ cups sweetened condensed milk

$1^1/_2$ teaspoons vanilla extract

$1^1/_2$ cups flour

3 teaspoons baking powder

Cream butter and sugar together; beat in eggs, one at a time. Pour in condensed milk; mix well. Add vanilla. Sift together remaining dry ingredients; stir into creamed mixture, a little at a time, beating after each addition until smooth. Spread batter in 2 greased and floured 9 x $1^1/_2$ inch round cake pans. Bake in moderate 375°F oven for 25 minutes. Place pans on wire rack; cool for about 30 minutes before removing cake from pans. Cut each layer into 2 layers. Spread each of the 3 layers with Cream Filling. Frost top of cake with Chocolate Glaze.

Cream Filling
1 envelope unflavored gelatin

1 cup cold water

$^2/_3$ cup sweetened condensed milk

$^1/_4$ teaspoon salt

2 eggs, slightly beaten

$1^1/_2$ teaspoons vanilla extract

1 cup heavy cream, whipped

Soften gelatin in cold water in top of double boiler; stir in condensed milk, salt, and eggs. Cook over simmering water for 10 minutes until mixture thickens. Remove from heat; cool over ice water. (Let mixture cool until it mounds slightly.) Fold in vanilla and whipped cream. Spoon between cake layers. Yields 3 cups.

Chocolate Glaze
2 (1 ounce) squares unsweetened
    chocolate

$^1/_4$ cup butter

3 tablespoons milk

2 cups sifted confectioners' sugar

$^1/_8$ teaspoon salt

$^1/_2$ teaspoon vanilla extract

Melt chocolate in small saucepan over low heat. Blend in butter and milk; remove from heat. Add sugar, salt, and vanilla. Mix well. Yields about $2^1/_2$ cups.

Coffee Fruit Drops

HANCOCK SHAKER VILLAGE

Makes about 6 dozen cookies

Ingredients

2 cups peeled and finely
   chopped apple
1 tablespoon powdered instant
   coffee, dissolved in 1 cup water
1 cup sugar
½ cup shortening
1 cup raisins
1 teaspoon cinnamon
¾ teaspoon cloves
¾ teaspoon nutmeg
1 teaspoon vanilla
3 cups flour
1 teaspoon baking soda
¼ teaspoon salt
½ cup chopped walnuts

Cook apple, coffee, sugar, shortening, raisins, and spices in saucepan gently until apple is tender. Remove from heat and cool. Heat oven to 375°F. Add vanilla to cooked mixture. Blend flour, soda, and salt; stir in. Mix in nuts. Make drops by heaping teaspoonfuls on ungreased baking sheet. Bake for about 12 minutes.

A seeded raisin or nut placed on top of each cooky before baking makes a pretty cooky.

Above: this brick building at Hancock Shaker village is built along typical Shaker lines with thick walls, many windows, and dual, separate entrances for men and women.

Taffy

FRANCES HALL, HANCOCK SHAKER VILLAGE

Makes about 2-3 dozen twists

Ingredients
1 cup sugar

½ cup honey

⅛ teaspoon salt

1 tablespoon butter

Cook all the ingredients together until a ball is formed when dropped in cold water. Pour on buttered platter until cool enough to pull. Butter hands and pull until hard twisting taffy for an attractive finish. All taffy takes two people to pull unless you have a hook set in the wall to secure one end of the taffy. When taffy is cool cut with scissors and wrap in paper.

Above: the Shaker commercial seed industry, begun at Mt. Lebananon, was the sect's most successful business.

Cranberry Relish

SHAKER FESTIVAL, AUBURN, KENTUCKY

Makes 8 cups

Ingredients

2 oranges
2 cups raw cranberries
3 sour apples

1 cup grated pineapple
2 cups sugar

Remove and discard peel from 1 orange. Put cranberries, oranges, and apples through coarse cut of food grinder. Add pineapple and sugar and let stand in cool place 6 hours before using. Do not cook.

Above: the Shakers concocted herbal medicines and developed a successful trade in such specialties as rose water, made from the roses grown in Shaker gardens.

India Relish

SOUTH UNION SHAKER VILLAGE, KENTUCKY

Makes 6-8 pints

Ingredients

8 pounds very small green tomatoes
8 cups brown or maple sugar
2 cups water
3 sticks cinnamon
2 tablespoons ginger

3 lemons, cut very thin
2 cups shredded citron
3 cups seedless raisins
Peel 1 small orange

Wash tomatoes and cut in quarters. Make syrup of sugar and water. Add tomatoes, cinnamon, ginger, lemons, citron, raisins, and orange peel. Boil slowly until fruit is clear and thick. Pour into sterilized containers and seal. This is excellent with cold meat.

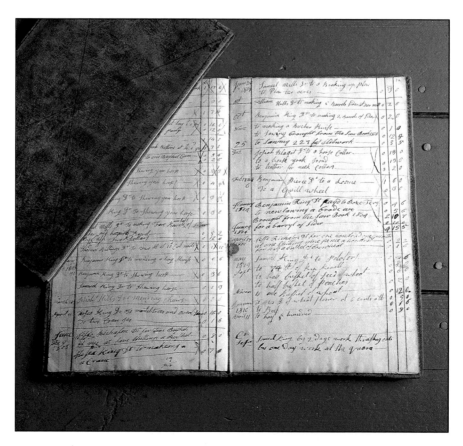

Above: day books from the Shaker community at Enfield, Connecticut indicate that the Shakers meticulously recorded the productivity of Brothers and Sisters.

Shaker Applesauce

MT. LEBANON SHAKER VILLAGE

Makes 2 pints

Ingredients

4 pounds apples, peeled
   and sliced thick
⅓ gallon Boiled Cider,
   boiled down from 1 gallon
   fresh cider

(1 cup sugar may be used
   in place of cider)

Add apple slices to boiled down cider; simmer until apples are tender. Do not stir, for apple slices must remain whole. Add sugar, if desired, but the concentrated cider is very sweet. Put in sterilized jars.

Above: the Shakers marketed some of their best wholesome produce during the 19th century when much commercial canning was unsanitary and unsafe.

Picnic Lemonade

MT. LEBANON SHAKER VILLAGE

Serves 16

Ingredients
12 lemons
1¼ cups sugar

3 quarts spring water
Mint sprigs

Lemons should be at room temperature. Roll to soften. Squeeze and remove pips but not fruit pieces. Add sugar and water. Stir well to dissolve. Taste and add more sugar if need be. Chill well.

Carry additional ice in blocks to the picnic. Pour lemonade from canteen, add mint sprigs. Stir well and ladle into little tin cups.

Above: Shakertown at Pleasant Hill, Kentucky has been carefully restored to its former glory as one of the largest and most impressive Shaker villages.